an
Edwardian
Family Album

A photographic portrayal of a Wirral
family in the early 20th century

David and Heather Price

Copyright © 2009 **Alyn Books** Ltd, The Nook, Pentre Road, Cilcain, Mold, Flintshire CH7 5PD.

ISBN 978-0-9559625-4-7

Editing: Lorna Jenner

Design: William Smuts

Printed by: Gomer Press, Llandysul, Ceredigion

With special thanks to my best friend Caroline Johnson for her help and support

This book is for Dai. It was something he planned to do after he retired when he would have the time. I wish he could have been here to do it for himself. It was always his ideal to share his love of photography and images with others and this is a perfect way to achieve his aim.

Foreword

The images reproduced in this book are selected from a collection of over 500 glass negatives that were found in the cupboard under the stairs of a house in Bebington. The family featured in the photographs had lived in the house for 42 years, from the 1930s to 1979. Prior to that we believe they lived in Rock Ferry and the images span a 30 year period mostly taken from the early 1900s to the 1930s. The last family member, Mary, left the house to her housekeeper who in turn sold it to the people who discovered the negatives in 1983. When enquiries failed to locate any further members of the family the negatives were given to David Price.

David, known as Dai to his friends, was renowned for his interest in the history of photography and old images. He had been a keen photographer since his childhood and his interest had expanded to include all aspects of photography including the history. He was a member of the Photographic Collectors Club of Great Britain, which further fuelled his interest. Over the final 25 years of his life he amassed a collection of all things photographic, from cameras and images, to darkroom equipment and chemicals.

When Dai first saw the negatives he was excited by diversity of subject matter and the quality of the images. As he spent time looking at and sorting them he developed an interest in the family as he felt that he had almost seen their children grow from babies to adulthood. He spent some time researching and, with the help of others, managed to get a brief family history.

Because of the special nature of the images, Dai was determined to share their content with as many people as possible. He began by showing some to work colleagues and, when he realised that their enthusiasm equalled his own, he took further steps by approaching the Lady Lever Gallery in Port Sunlight with a view to staging an exhibition. During the organisation of the exhibition Dai sadly passed away, but arrangements for the exhibition continued in his absence, bringing the images to a wider audience. This book contains a larger number of these wonderful photographs, including many of his favourite images. I hope you enjoy them as much as he did.

Heather Price

Contents

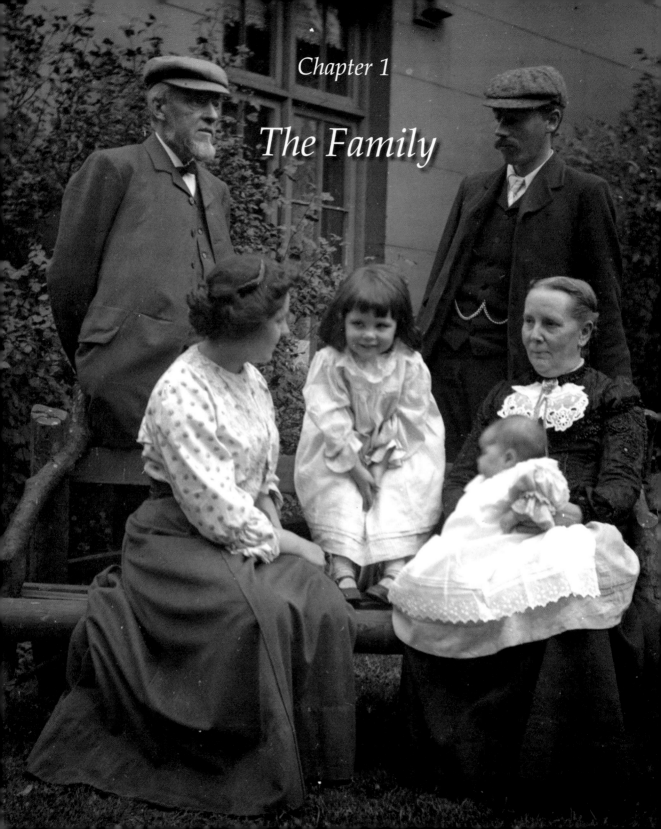

Chapter 1

The Family

This chapter introduces the Urton family who moved to the Wirral from Derbyshire at the beginning of the 20th century. Jack, the father, was born in Chesterfield in 1876 and was probably the keen photographer. He married his wife Biddy in 1897, and they had two daughters, Mary who was born in 1903, and Lois who was born in 1906. Their son, Harold, was born in 1898 but died, aged five.

Jack died at the age of 64 but Biddy survived him by 18 years, living to 82. Lois lived to 62 and Mary to 76 years. Neither Mary nor Lois married and all attempts to find other relatives in the area have failed. The family grave can be found in Bebington cemetery.

The negatives give a fascinating insight into the lives of a 'middle class' family of the time. The childhood of the girls is well documented through pictures from babyhood to adulthood. This era evokes the image of children being seen and not heard but that is certainly not evident from these images as there are delightful scenes of the children playing and their father enjoying spending time with them. I'm sure Jack would be pleased to think his photographs were being enjoyed 100 years on.

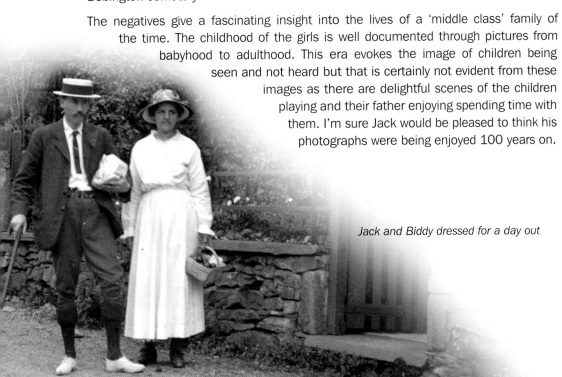

Jack and Biddy dressed for a day out

Mary in the playpen with the family dog

Mary

Opposite: Grandfather and Grandmother

Nancy and Mary in the barrow

In the greenhouse

Mary with Lois in the rocking horse

Jack and Mary - a touching scene between father and daughter

Lois

The family at a Christening party in Curbar, Derbyshire

Relaxing in the garden

Chapter 2

At the Seaside

The lure of the seaside seems to have been as great then as it is today as there are numerous images of the family enjoying themselves at nearby Wallasey and New Brighton. These day trips to the beach were serious undertakings, involving a vast amount of preparation, loading a tent, rugs, cooking utensils, food, buckets and spades etc onto an old pram that was pushed down to the beach. Mother cooked food on a campfire - barbeques were yet to come. In addition to the favourite beach activities of paddling and building sandcastles, kite flying was evidently a passion too!

Flying kites at New Brighton

In 1909 a trip to the beach at Wallasey was a serious affair - the wagon is loaded with everything needed for a day out

The wagon is unloaded and a tent erected

The family gathers for lunch

Mother, Lois and Mary searching for shells

Father paddling with the girls at Wallasey

New Brighton seafront, showing the tower that was demolished in 1919.

*Opposite: Washing
the dog*

Father gets wet too

Building a sand castle with a moat for the yachts needs careful supervision

Kite party at New Brighton

Flying kites at New Brighton

Even the girls have a turn

There was a selection of kites to choose from

Chapter 3

At Home

The images in this chapter evoke an active and happy household. Many are taken in the garden, showing the family working on the vegetable plot, apple picking and chopping wood, but others show them relaxing and playing. The girls can be seen helping out with the more mundane household tasks as well as feeding ducks and chickens. They were fond of dressing up and there are several images depicting them in costumes and others that may have been taken for Christmas cards. Pets, especially the dogs, were obviously important family members as they feature in many of the photographs, both at home and on many of the outings and holidays.

Mother and Lois feeding the ducks

Mother and children chopping kindling

Opposite: Mother and Mary apple picking

Helping Grandmother pick cabbages

Looking after the duck or the garden?

The girls with their pets

Mary with some of her dolls

A much-loved dog

Father with his two girls

Mary busy on wash day

Illicit activities in the scullery

Representing the 4 nations of Britain - Wales, England, Ireland and Scotland

A Dutch girl?

Trying on the workman's clothes

Image for a Christmas card?

Another Christmas wish - 1910

Chapter 4

On Holiday

Holidays seemed to take the family back to their roots in Derbyshire although there are other images, not included here, of North Yorkshire and Northumberland. Many of the locations are named, although Jack's handwriting on the glass negative sleeves was sometimes difficult to interpret. Finding the actual locations on maps has proved a challenge in some cases.

They were an active group, often travelling with friends and family, with plenty of cycling and walking. Picnicing was a popular activity and the picnic blanket and basket are often seen in the pictures along with the kettle, stove and teapot.

At the Botanical Gardens

The boathouse at Lathkil Dale

Beyond the bridge at Lathkil Dale

Out for a walk in Derbyshire

Castleton Cave

Wellington Cross

Taking the view from Eagle Stone

Dove Dale, 1909

Chesterfield

Castleton, 1909

A thatched cottage in Derbyshire

Stepping Stones on the Derwent

Porth Defarch, Holyhead

The river bed at Derwent

Peak Cavern

*Opposite: Waterfall, most
likely at Derwent*

Miner's Arms Pub

Chatsworth House

Chapter 5

Out and About

They must have been an outdoor-loving family as there are numerous images of picnics, walks, tennis and scout activities. Jack seems to have enjoyed hunting and shooting, and his prowess is confirmed with him proudly showing off his trophy from the Oxton Rifle Club. Fishing also seemed popular, with the whole family taking part and they also happily joined in helping with the haymaking!

The girls on the water

A picnic with the McLachlan children, 1910

The ladies go ahead to make tea at Cordwell

Fishing reflections

All the family enjoyed fishing

The girls inspect the contents of the net

Removing the hook

Anyone for tennis?

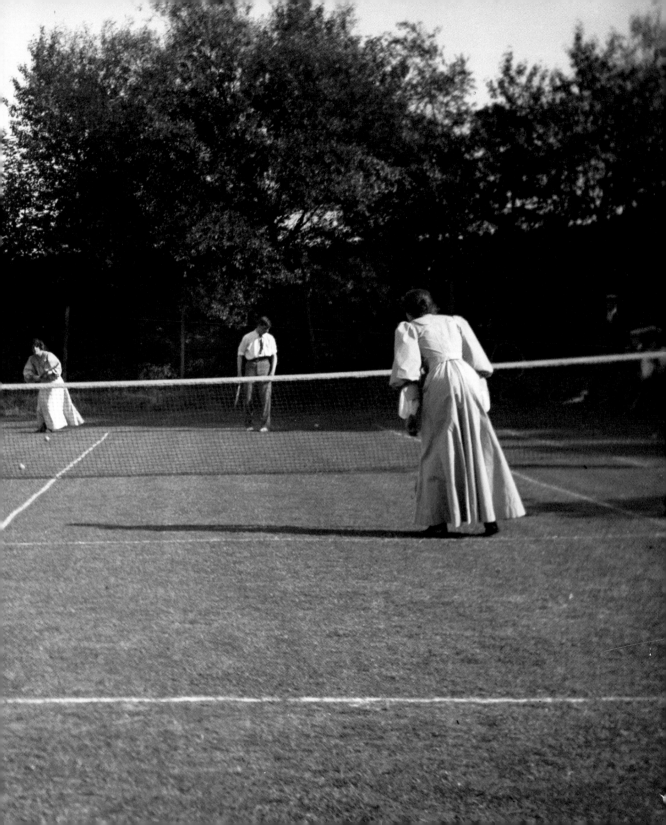

The family share a picnic in the country

Opposite: Jack with the Challenge Cup Trophy from Oxton Rifle Club

The family now grown up

A family outing in Holyhead

Out for a walk at Brookside

*Opposite: Haymaking in
Curbar, Derbyshire*

Chapter 6

On the Move

The evolution of the family transport is evident through the images in this collection. They start with the humble horse and graduate through bicycles, motorcycles and finish with the motorcar. The thought of travelling in the wicker basket sidecar on a motorcycle is quite horrifying and the consequences of things going wrong are well illustrated!

Cycling was a popular pastime

On horseback at Curbar

A day out for the family

Everyone used a bicycle

Even the children help cleaning the bicycles

The girls try out the motorbike and sidecar

Aunt Jane sits in the wicker basket sidecar

The first motorised vehicles

There's many a picnic during a trip out on the motor bikes - the new side car looks a bit sturdier

The whole family can fit in the new combination

Unfortunately these combinations aren't always very robust!

The new car is a convertible

The car is better for the less clement weather

Chapter 7

At Work

Research has shown that Jack started out as a draughtsman and became an engineer as his career progressed. The original family business in Chesterfield was the supply of agricultural machinery but, when Jack moved to the Wirral, he appears to have gone into the shipbuilding industry. There are many photographs of sea trials as well as images from the shipbuilding workshops and drawing office. A number of ships are named including the Cossack, Pathfinder and the Swift but attempts to link these vessels to the Wirral have failed. A number of pictures depicted the Cossack trials that took place on the Clyde so it may be that Jack travelled with his work.

The Iris from Wallasey

The family business in Derbyshire

HMS Pathfinder

Opposite: HMS Pathfinder
in dry dock

Claughton, a Woodside Ferry

Opposite: Aboard the Swift

Looking astern on the Cossack during trials

The deck of the Cossack during trials on the Clyde

A launching party, possibly at Cammell Lairds

The launched ship hits the water

An astern turbine at the shipyard

Branch	Date
TS	12/11